Nights Of Zendala

I0493305

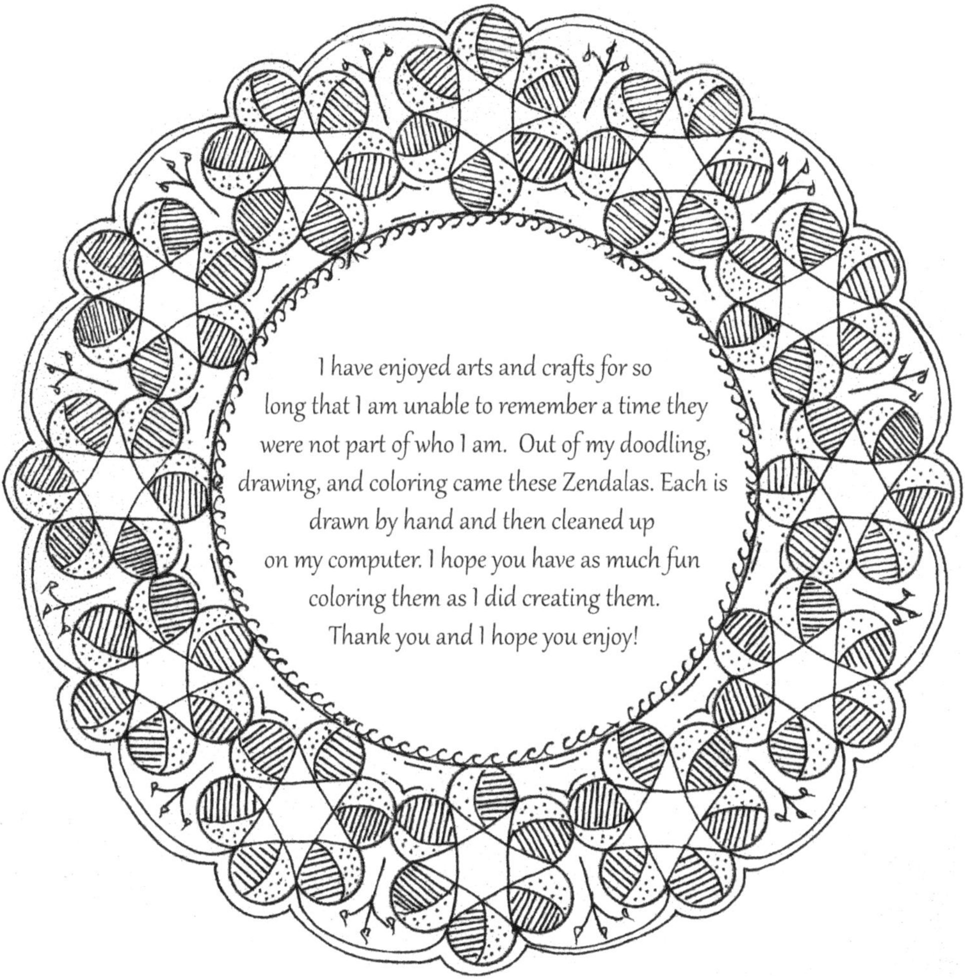

I have enjoyed arts and crafts for so
long that I am unable to remember a time they
were not part of who I am. Out of my doodling,
drawing, and coloring came these Zendalas. Each is
drawn by hand and then cleaned up
on my computer. I hope you have as much fun
coloring them as I did creating them.
Thank you and I hope you enjoy!

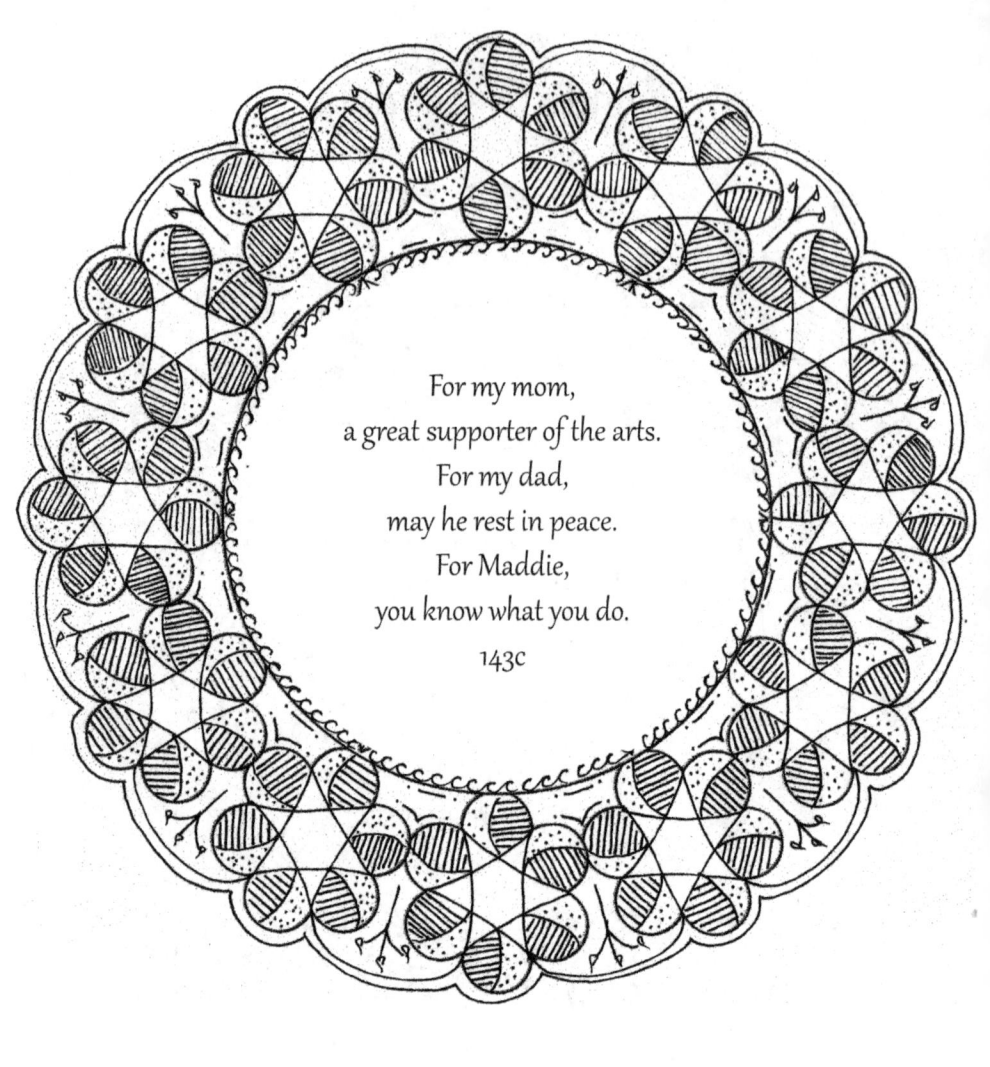

For my mom,
a great supporter of the arts.
For my dad,
may he rest in peace.
For Maddie,
you know what you do.

143c

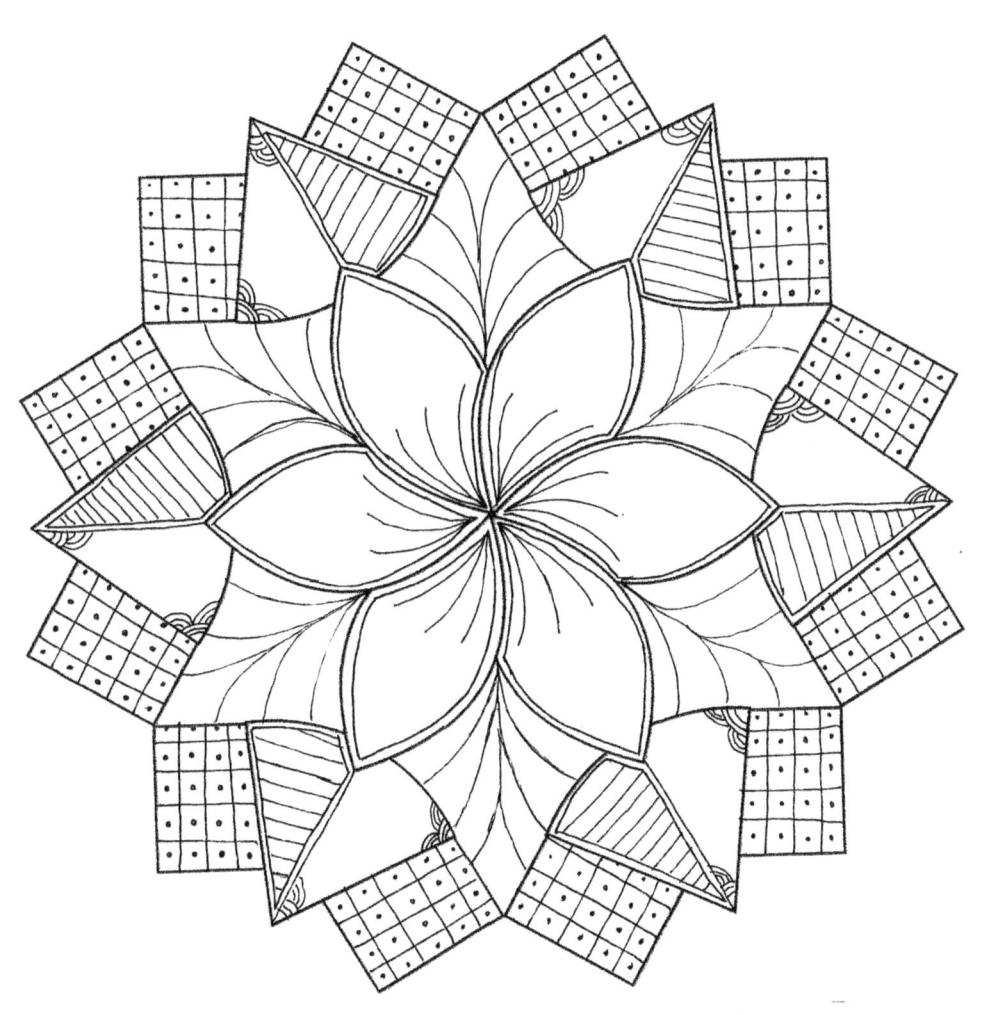

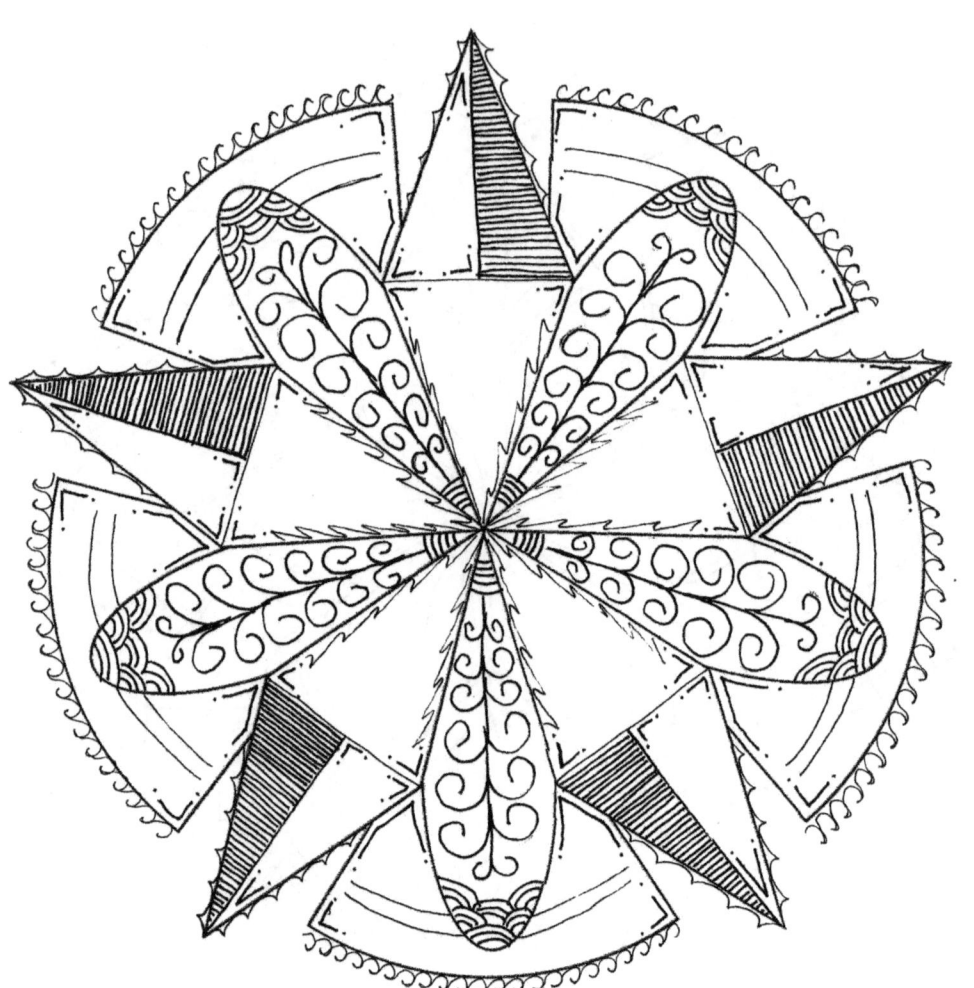

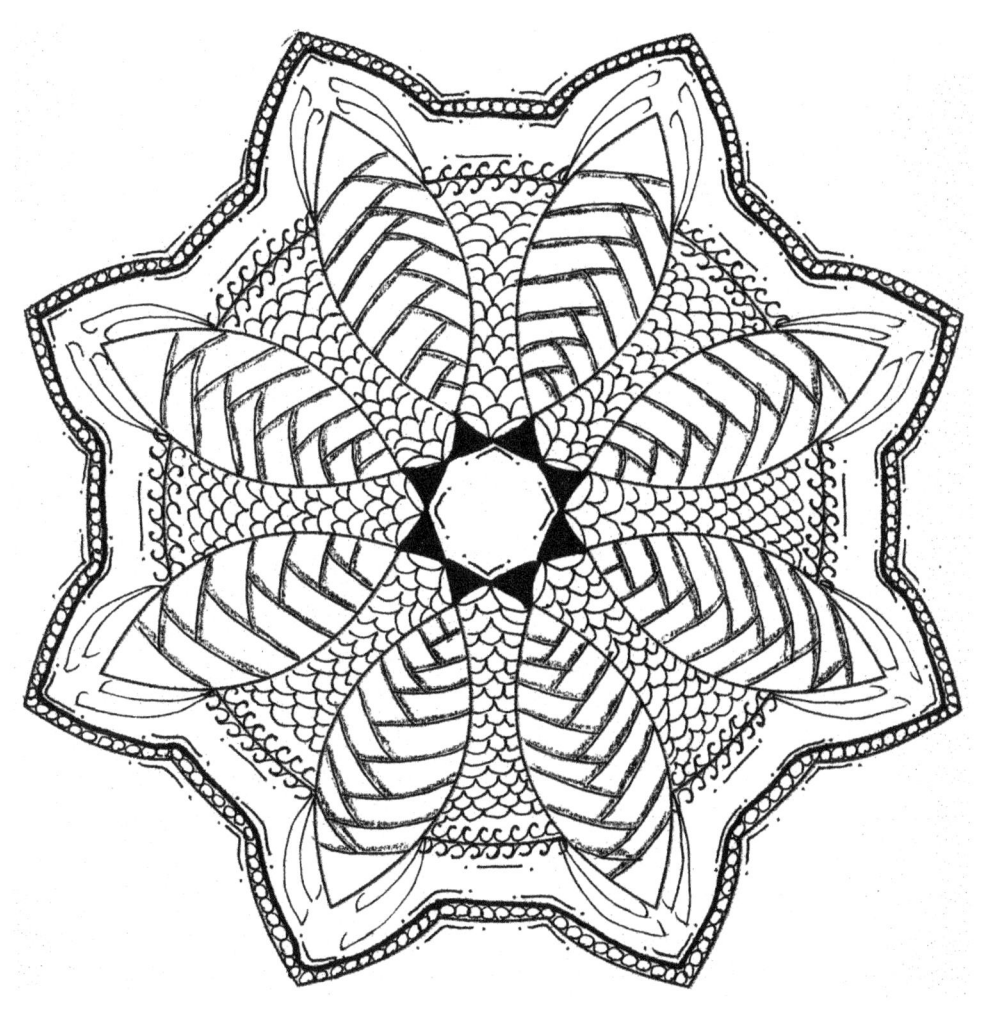

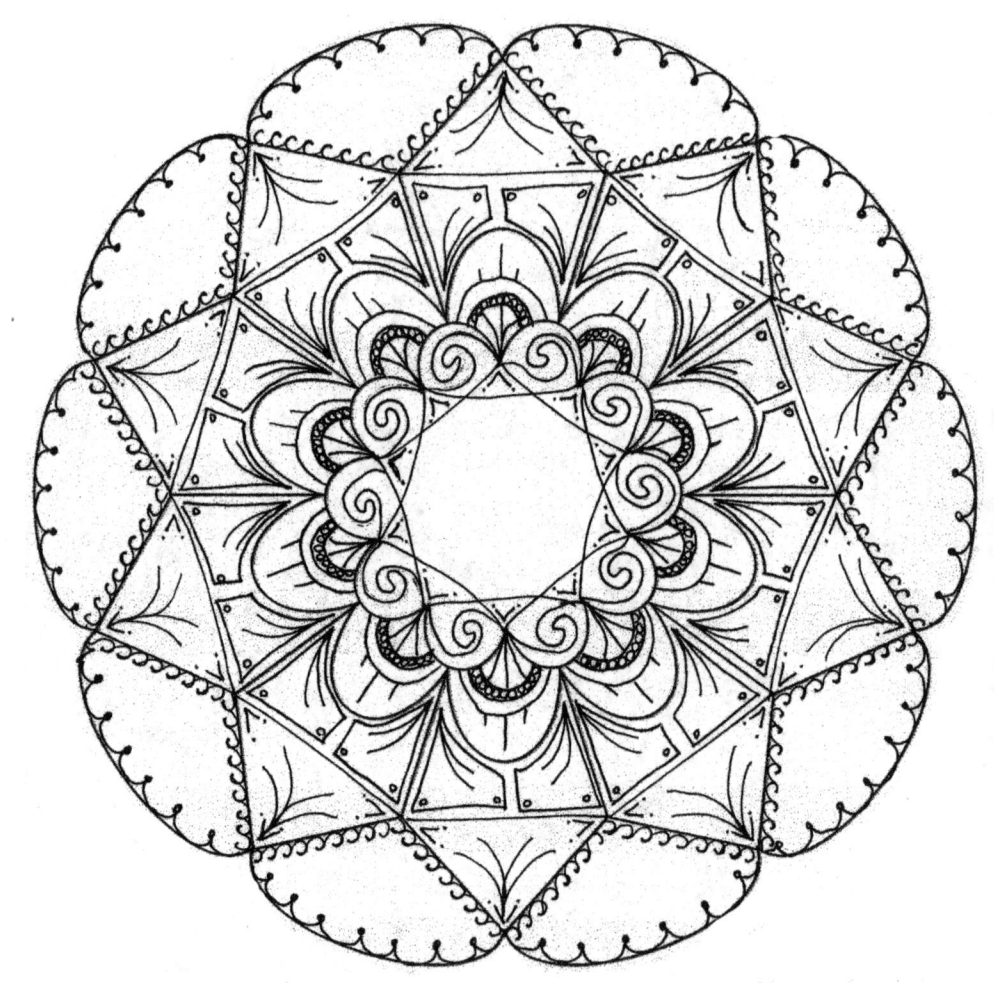

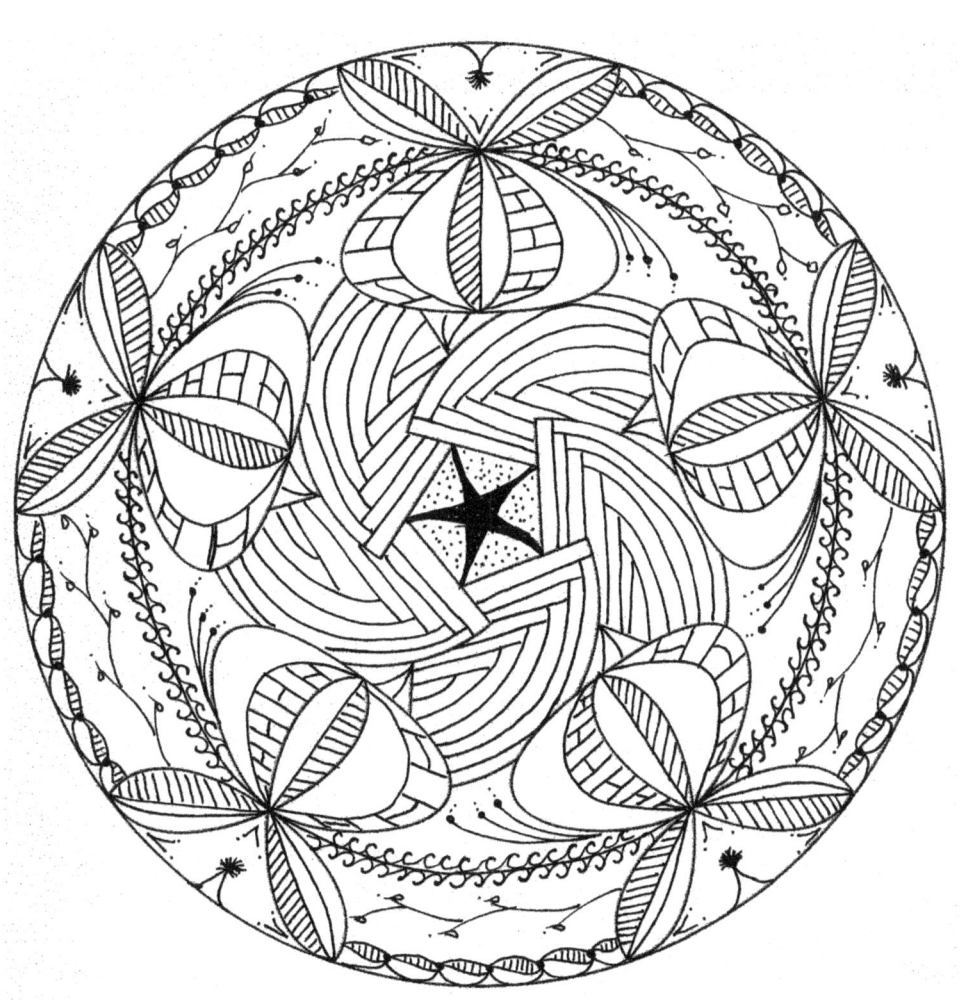

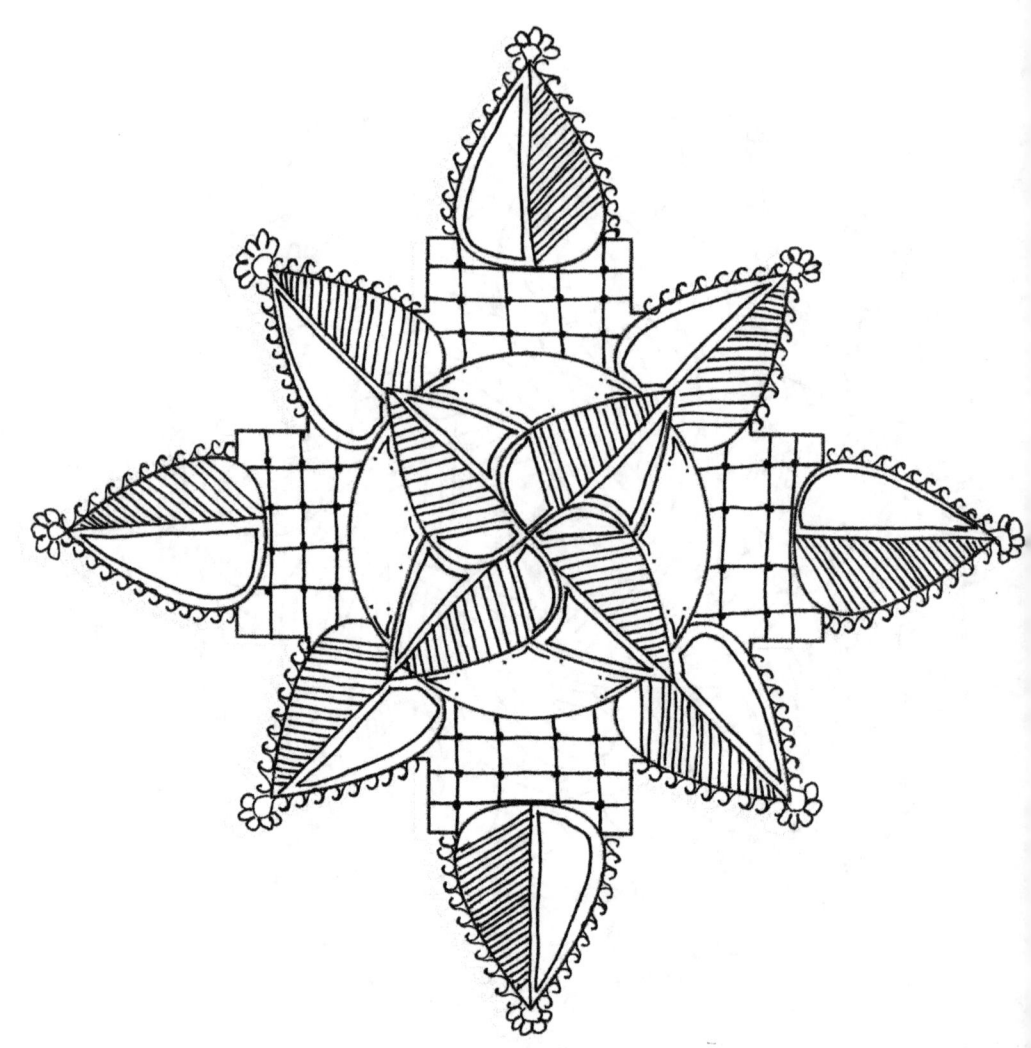

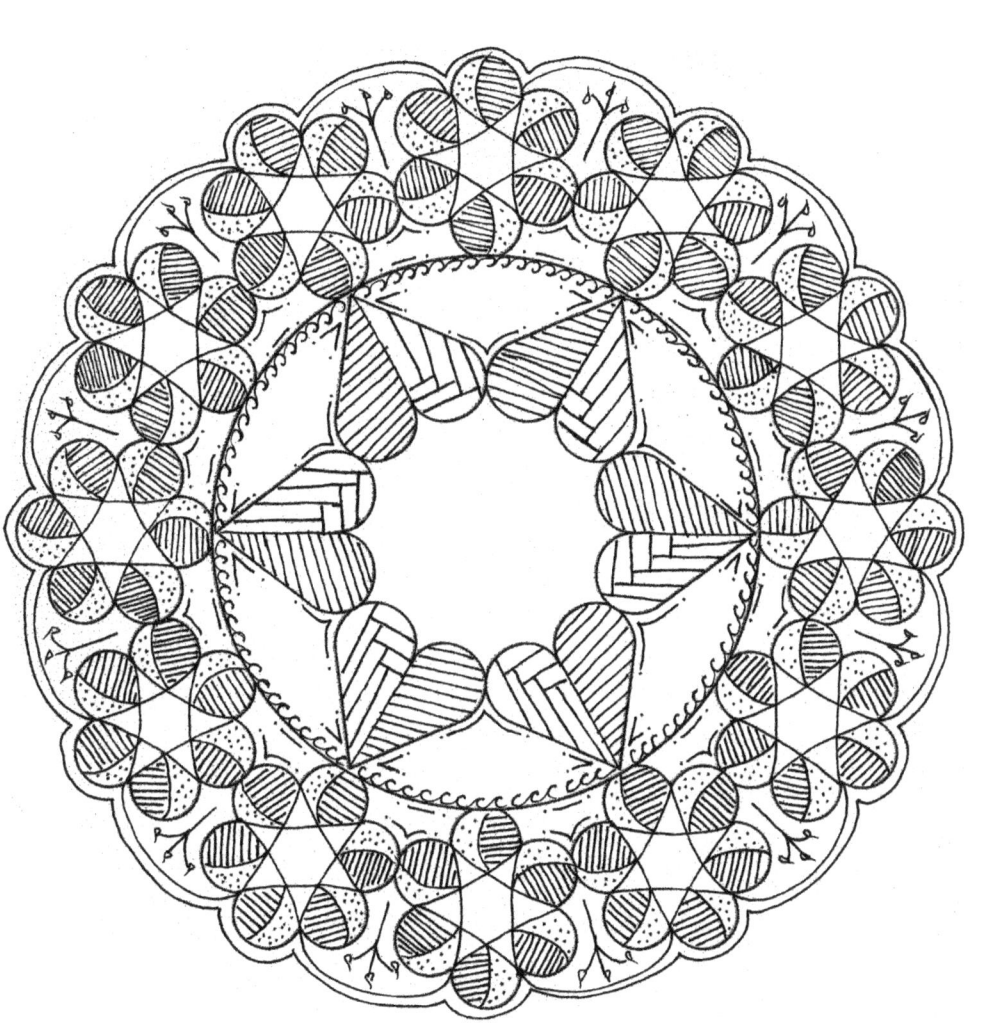

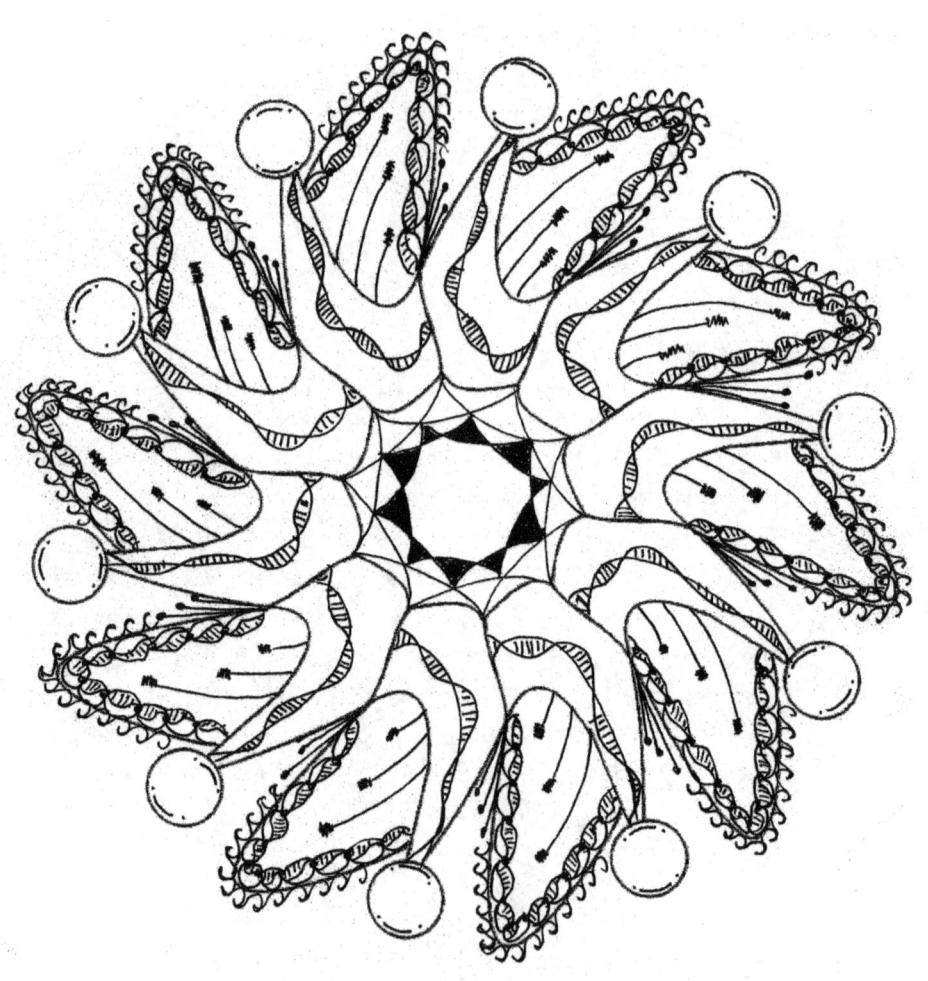

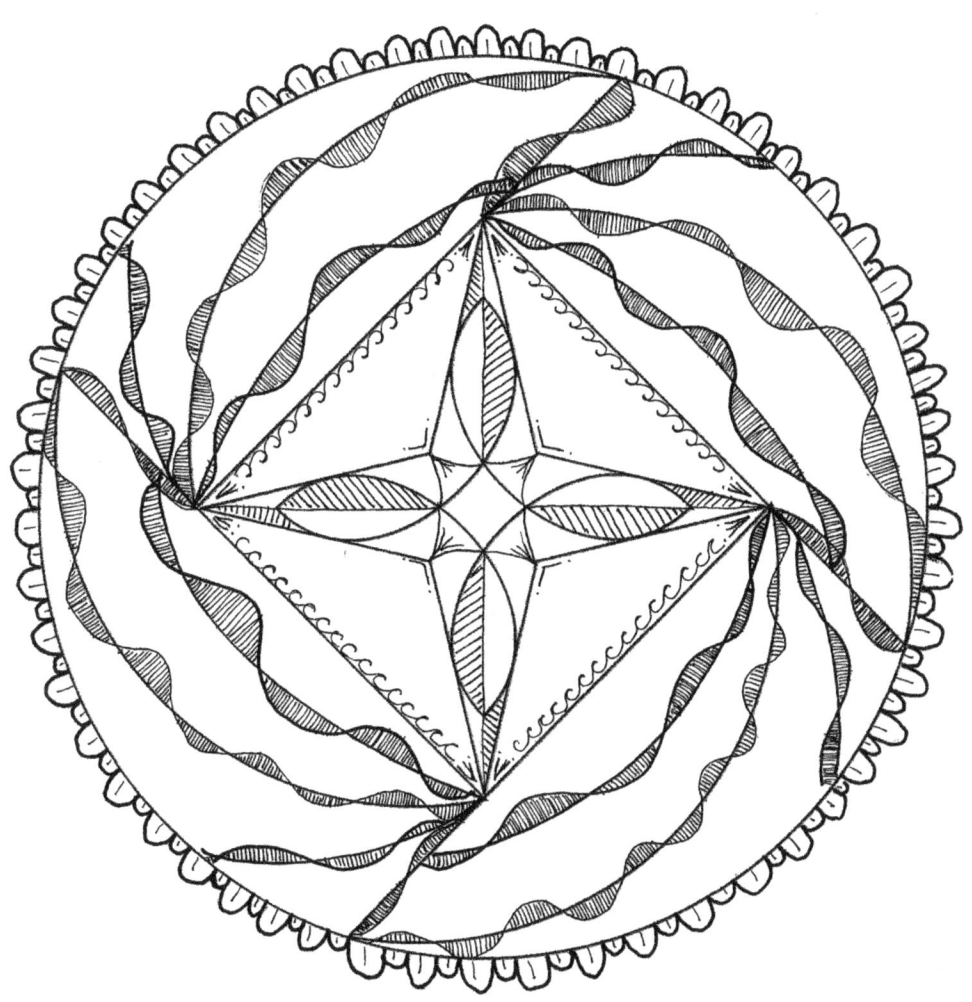

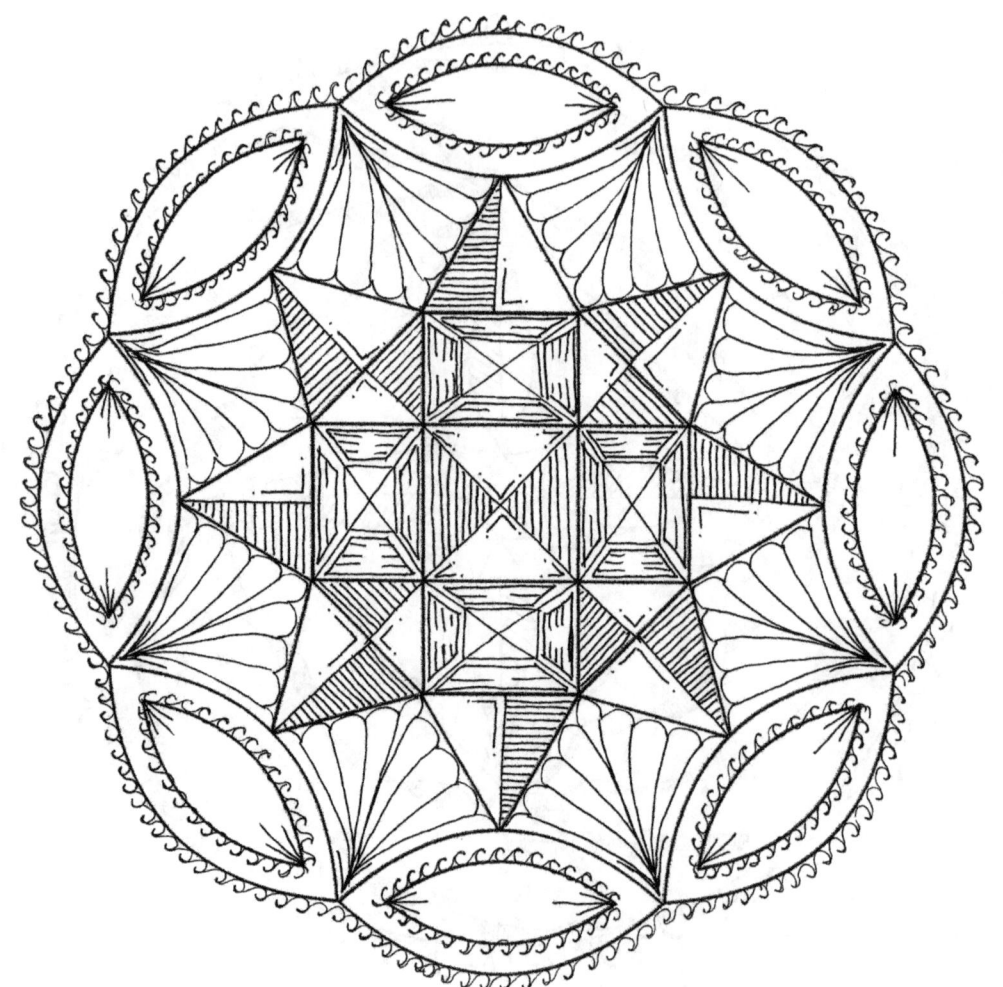

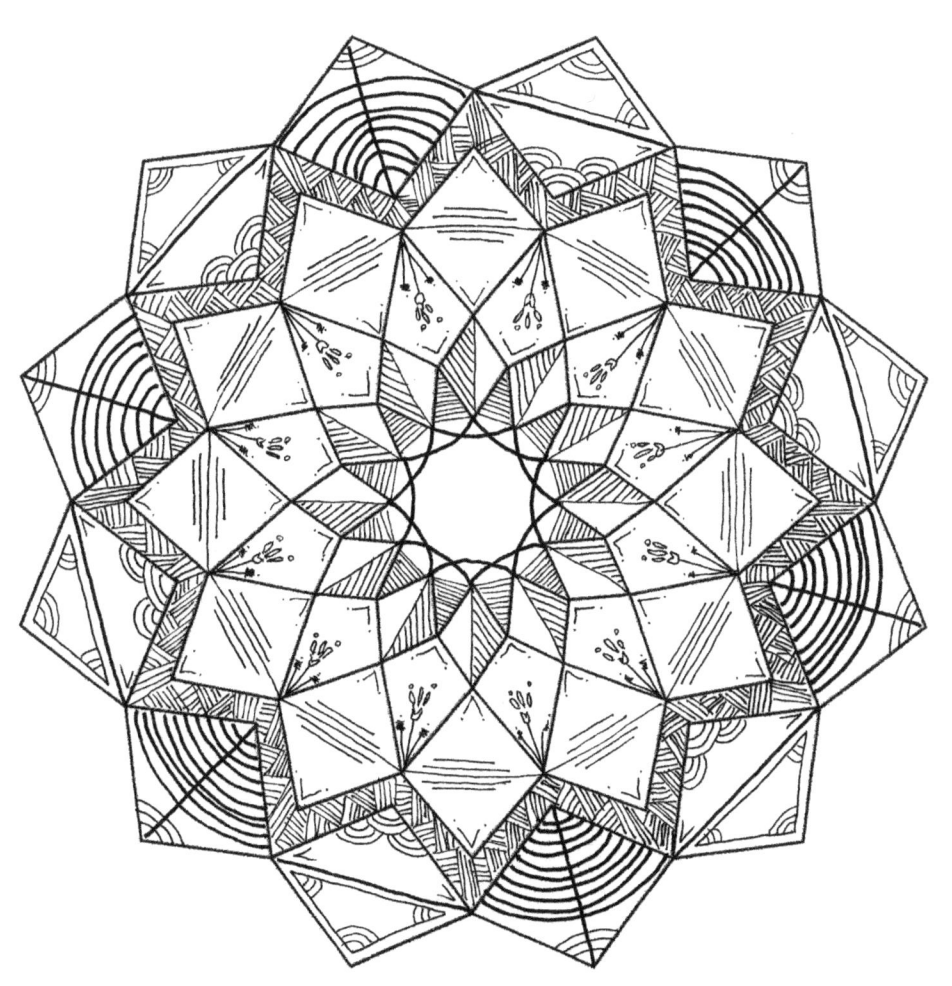

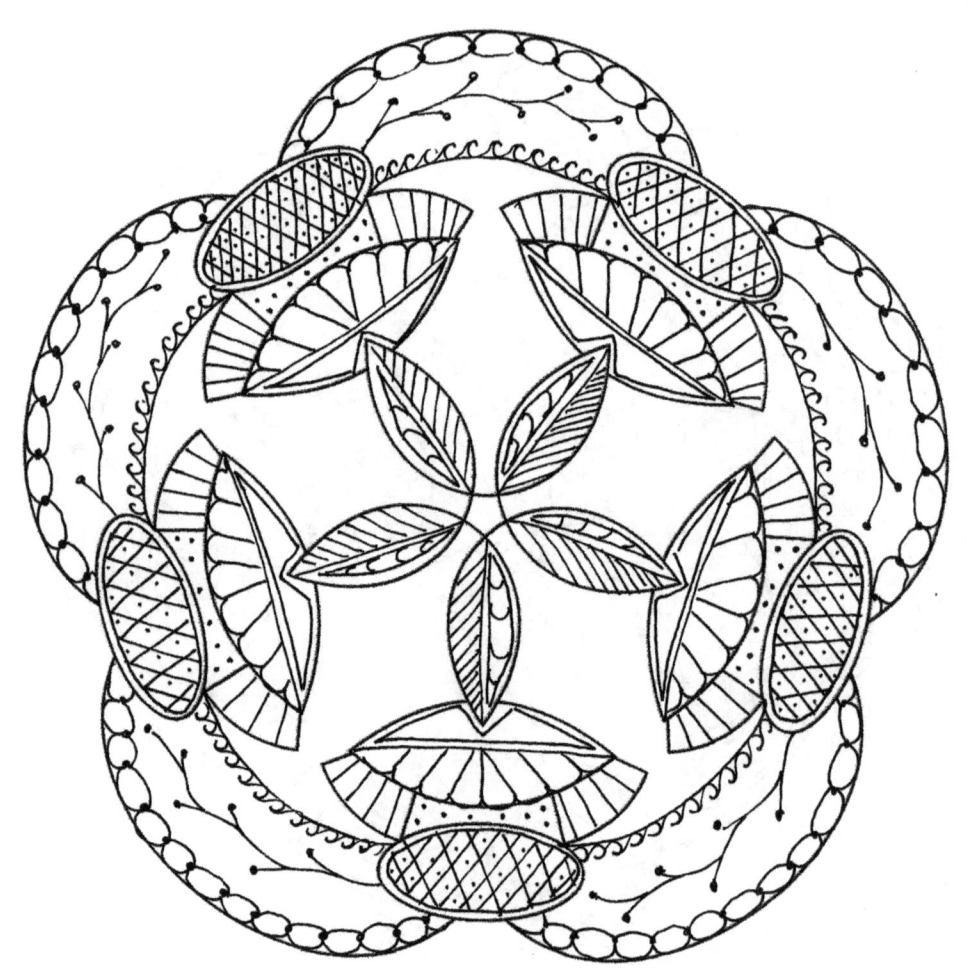

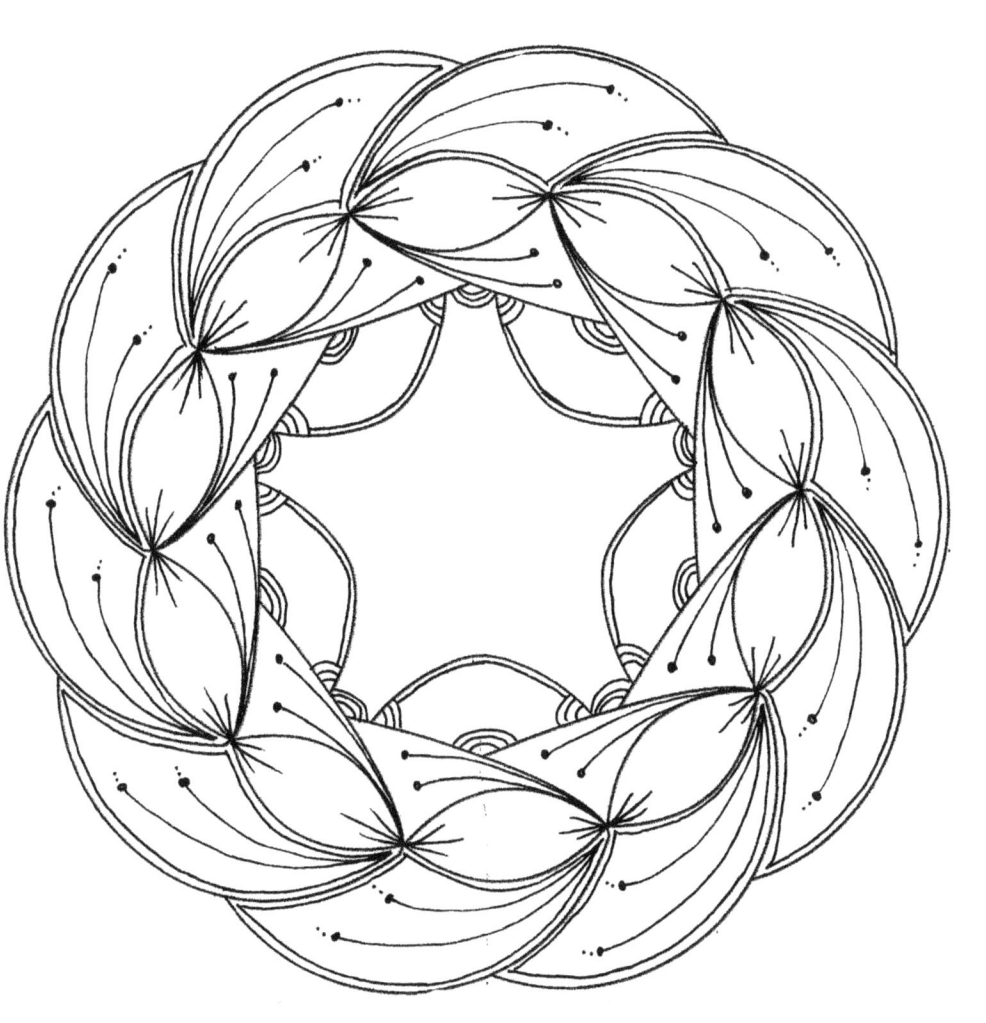

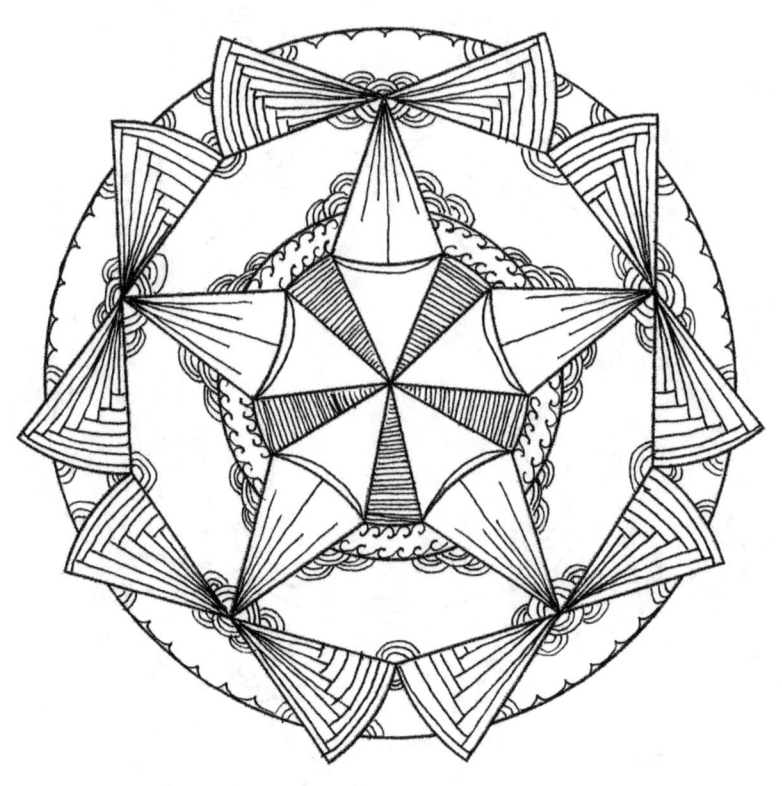

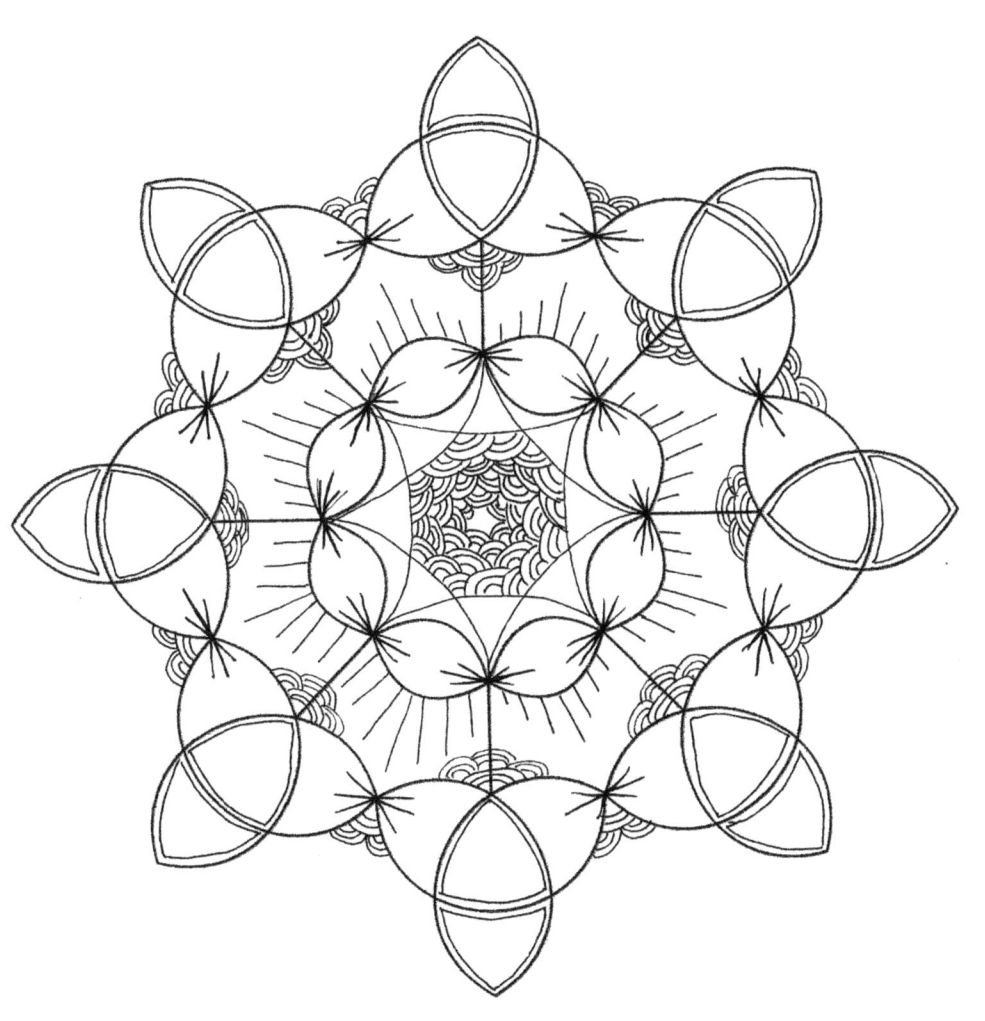

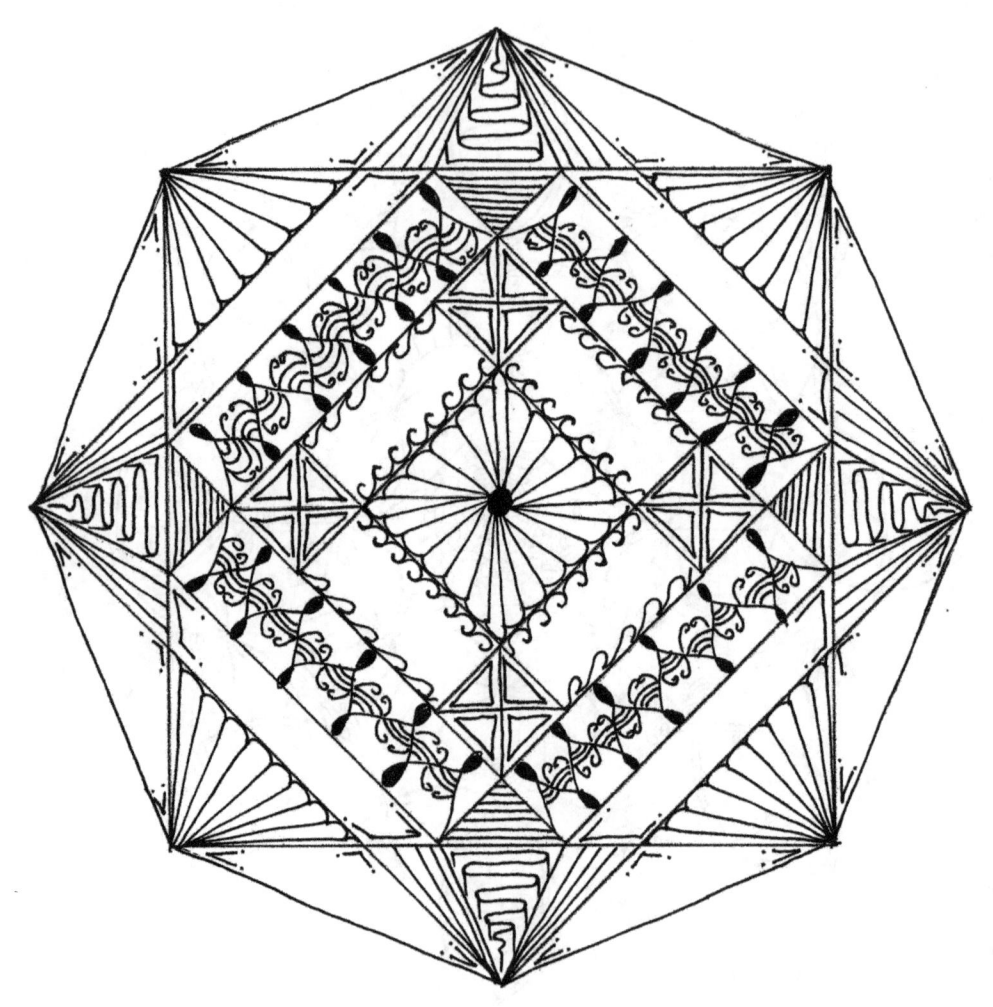

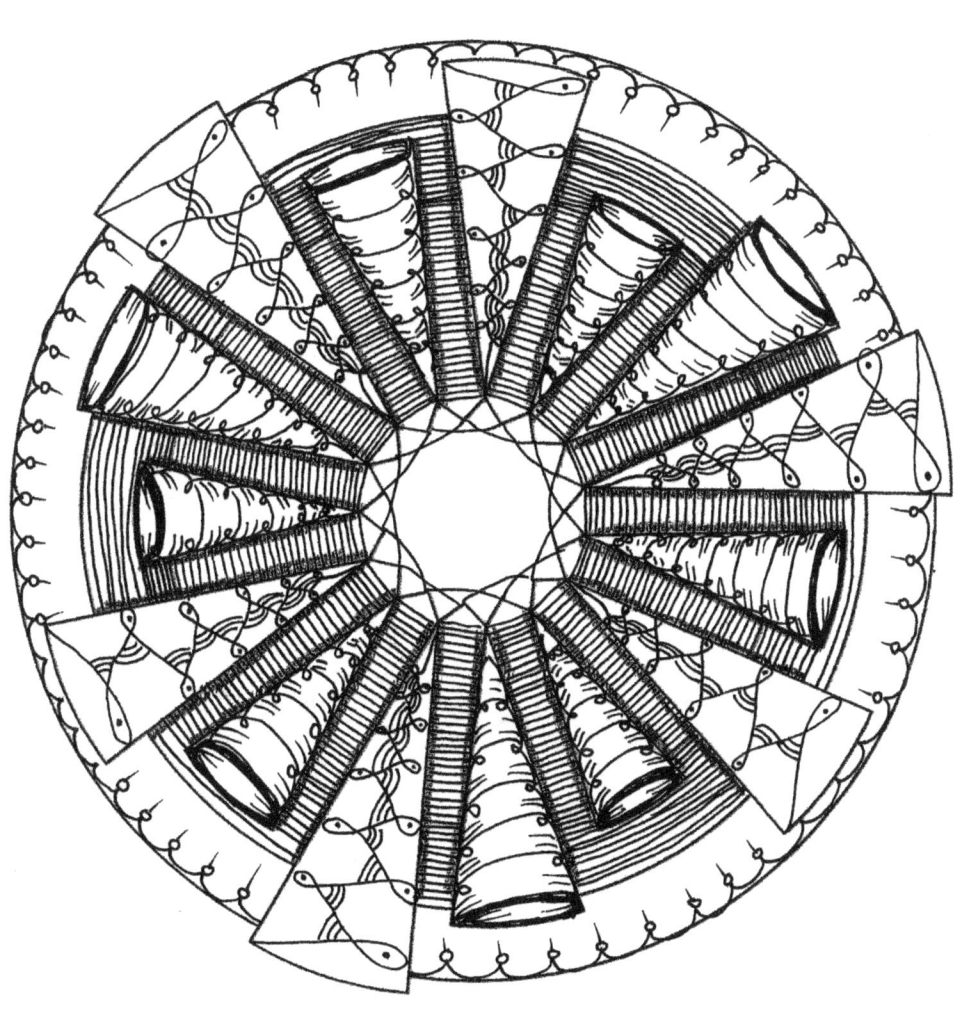

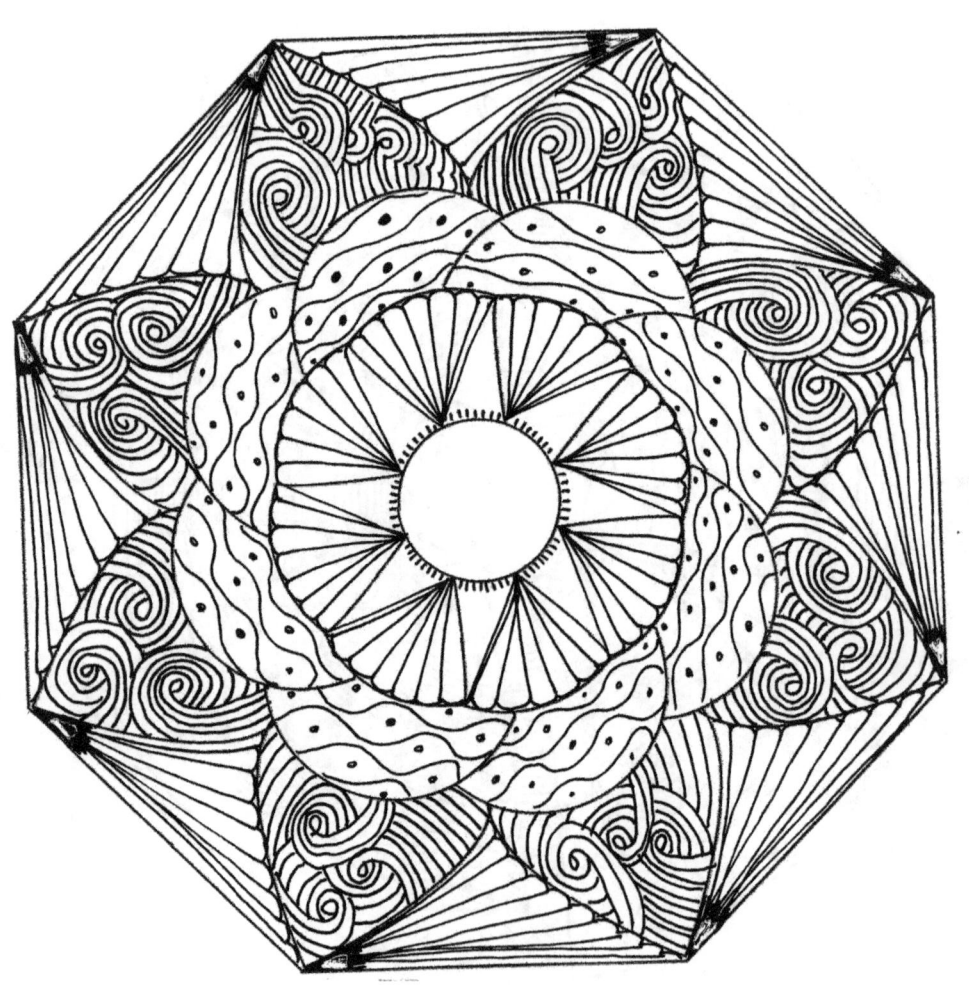

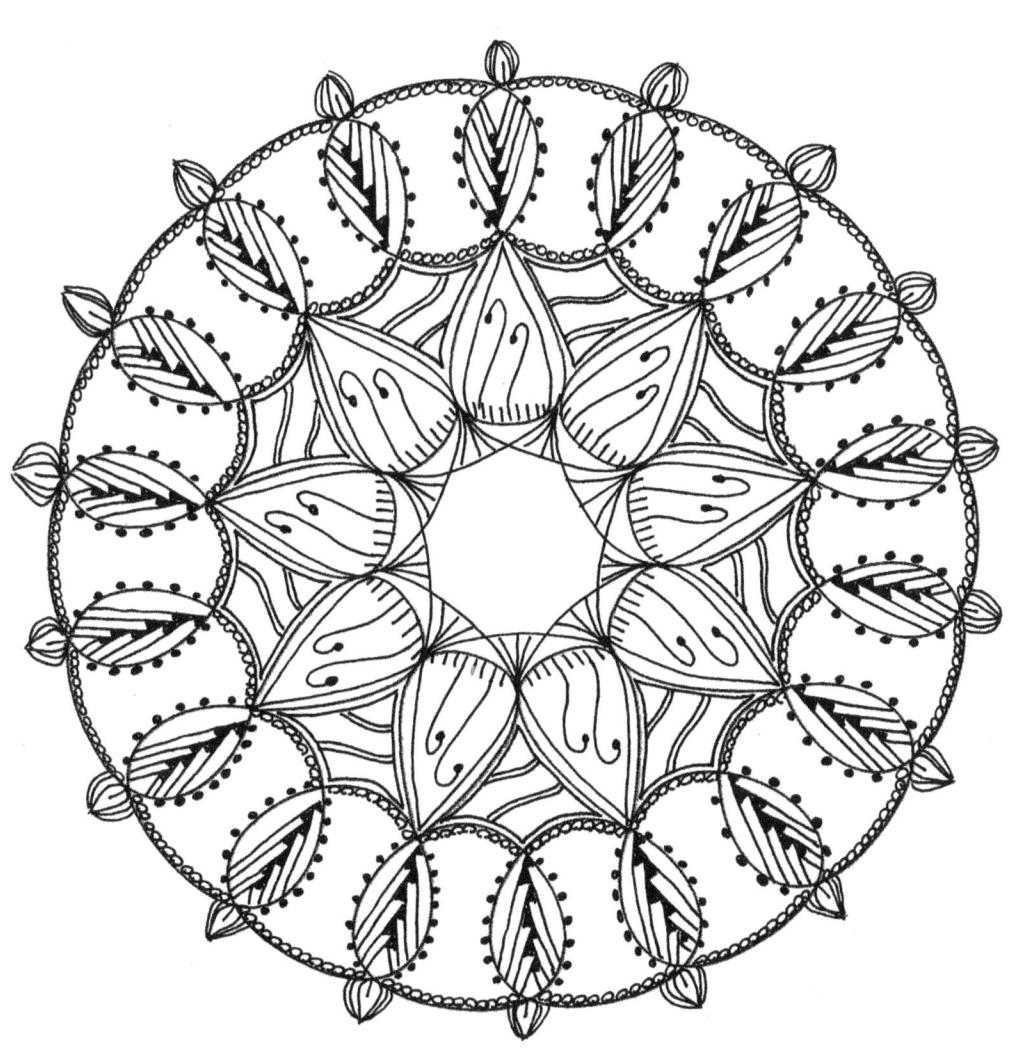

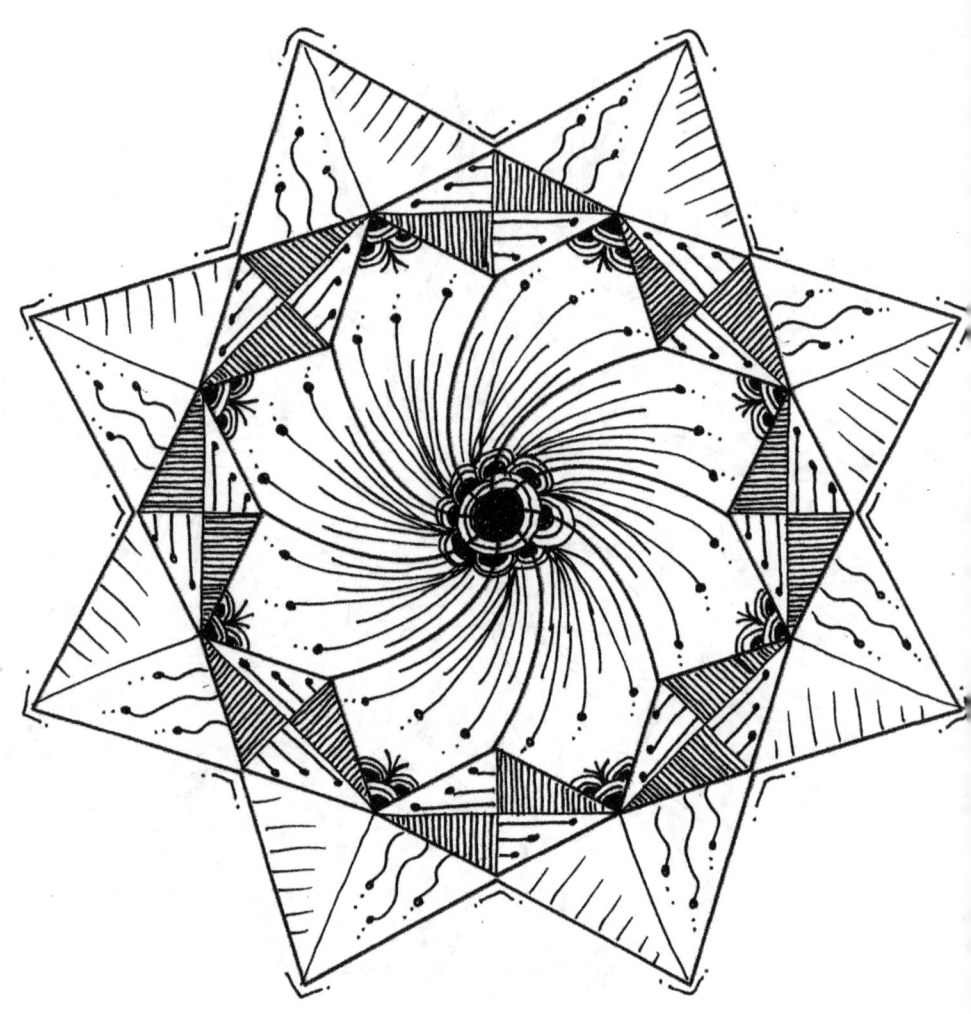

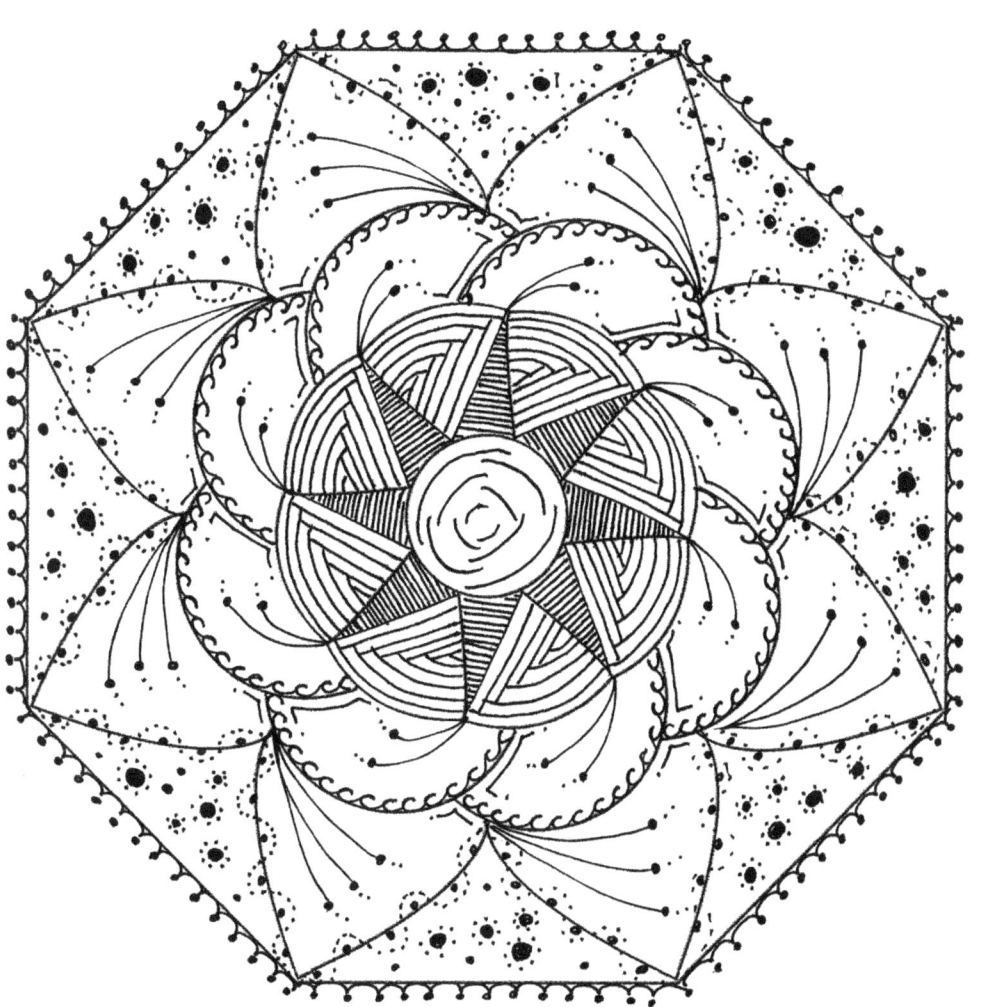

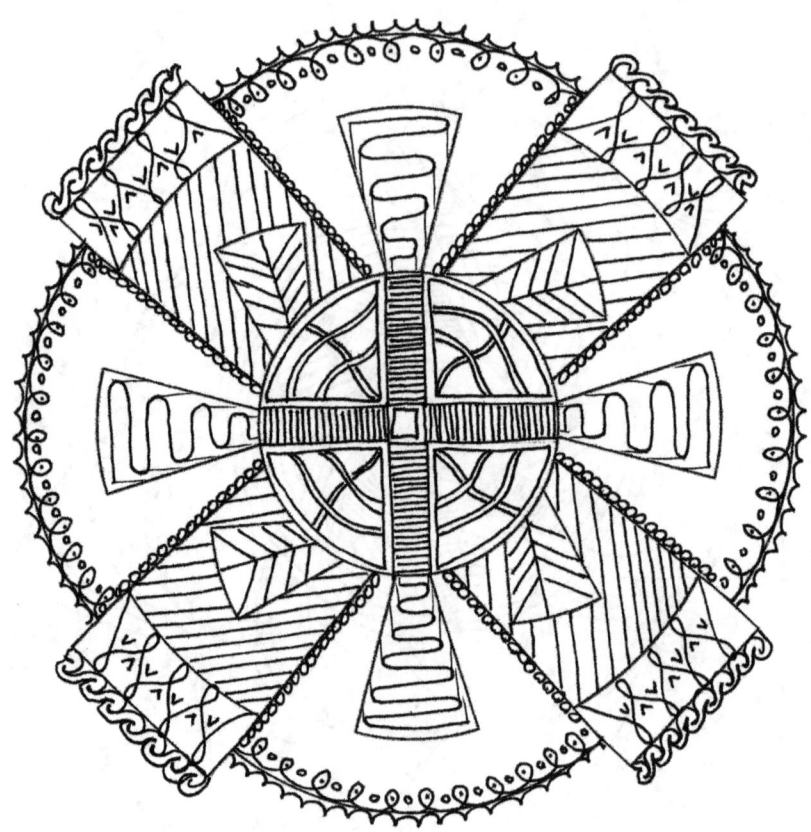

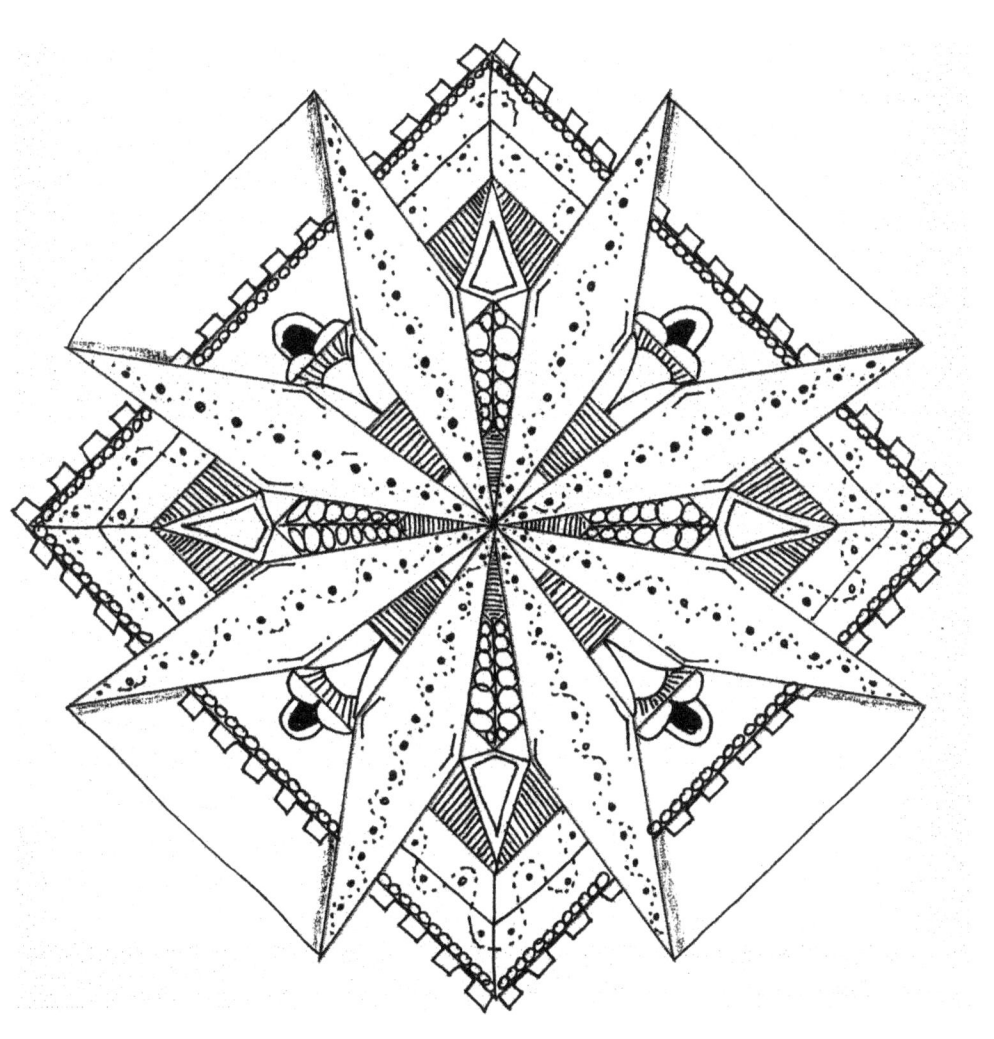

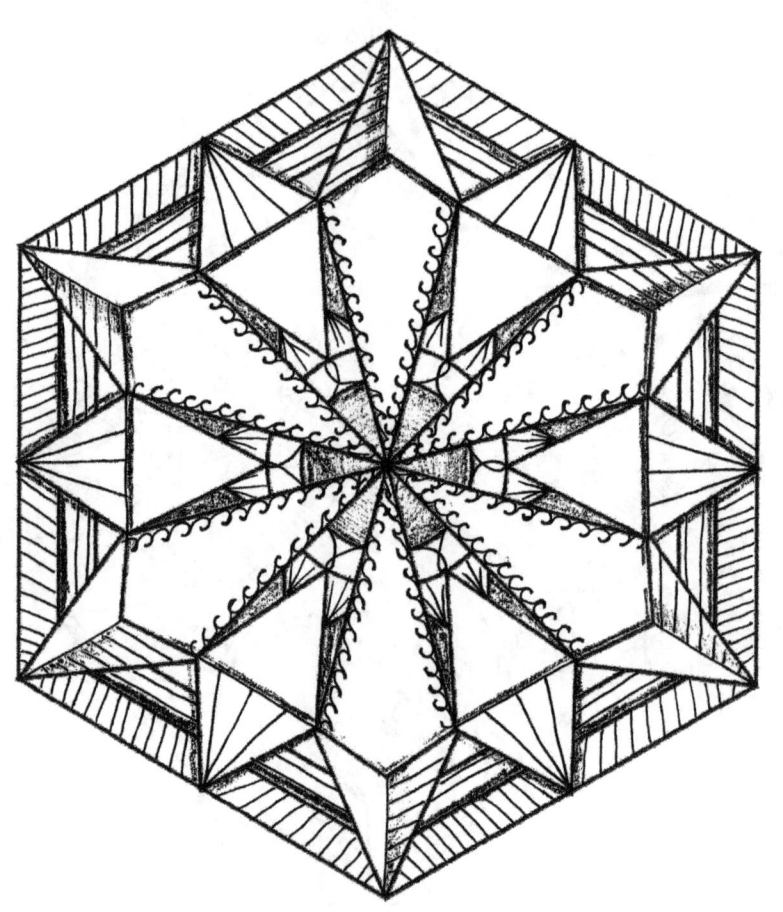

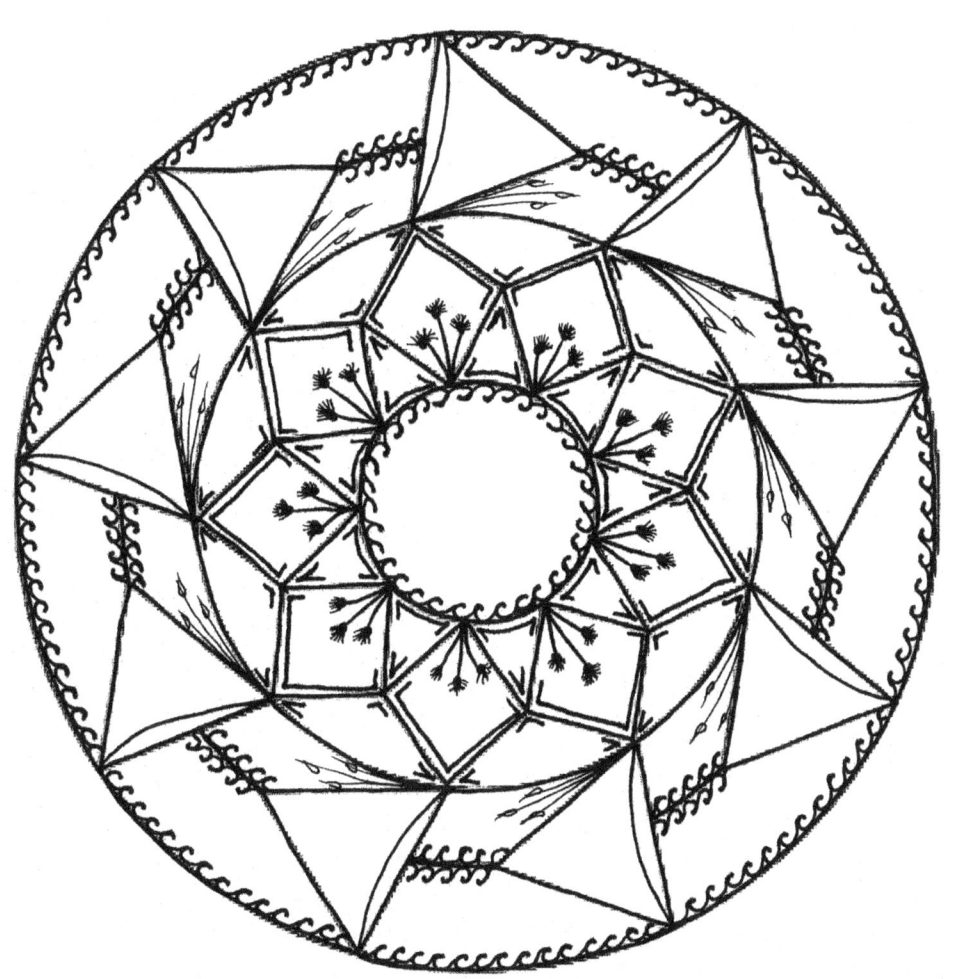

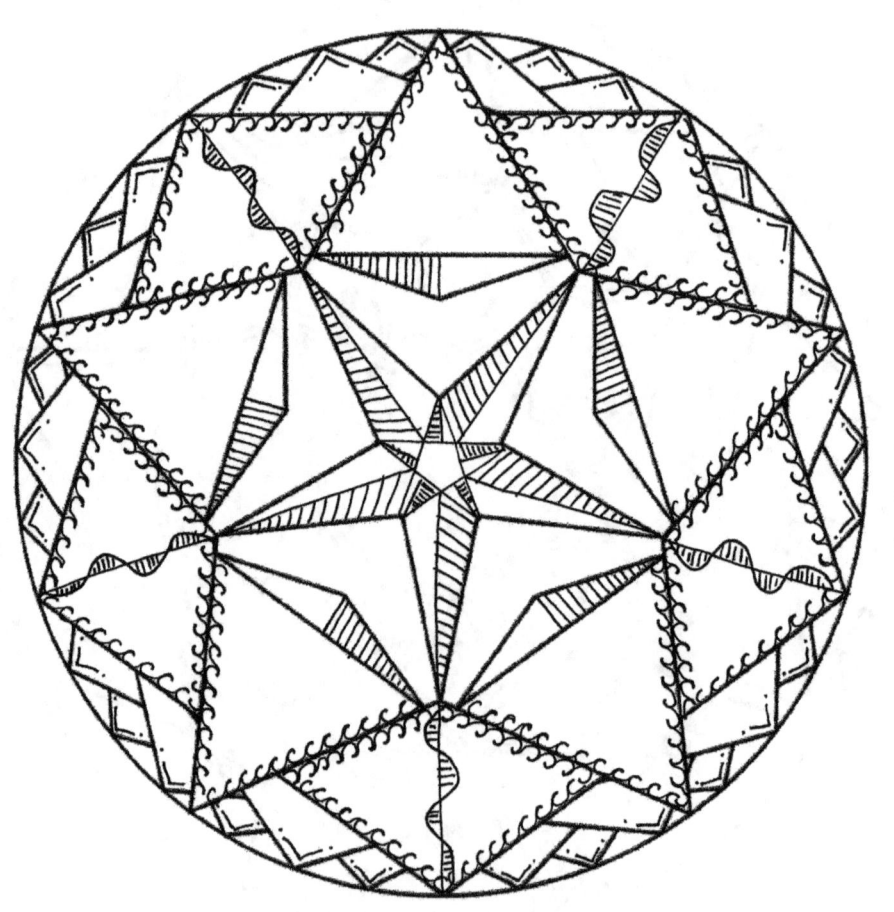

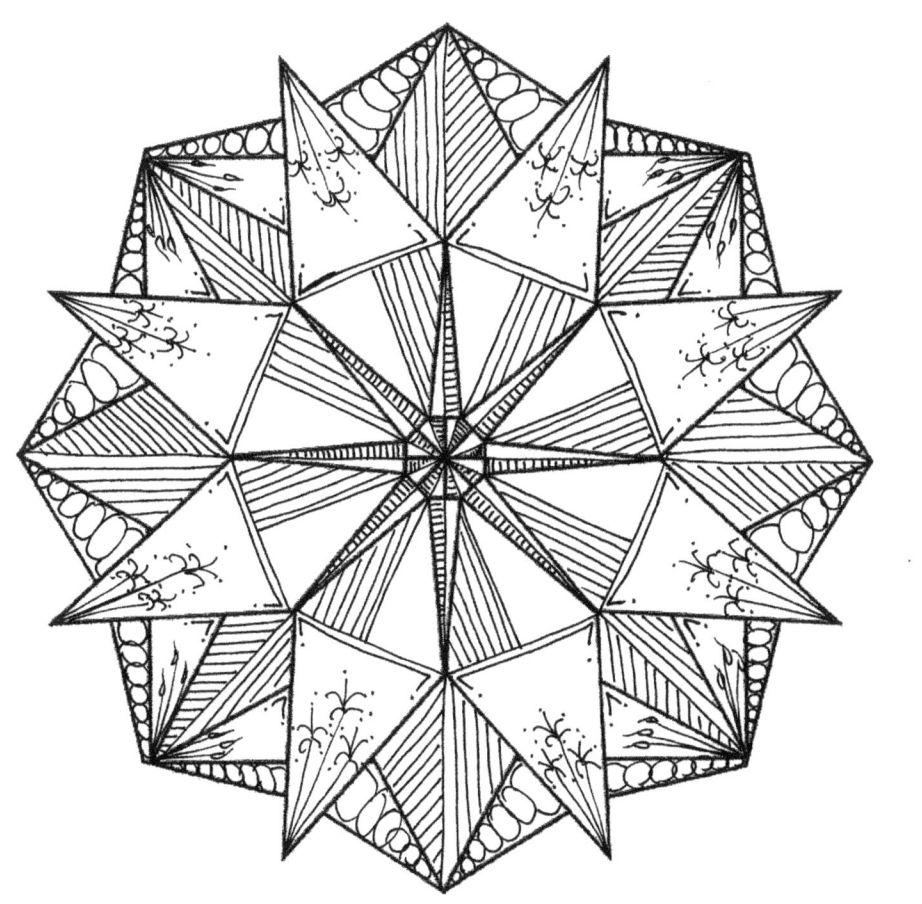

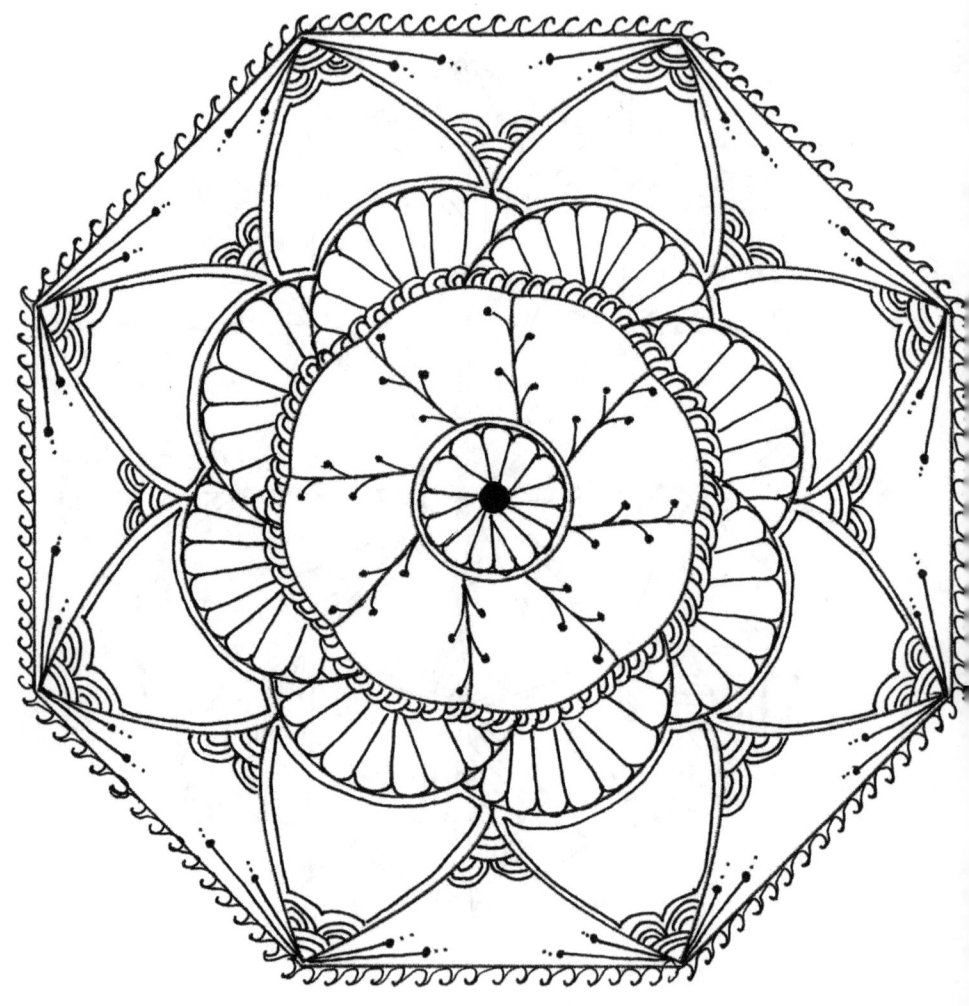

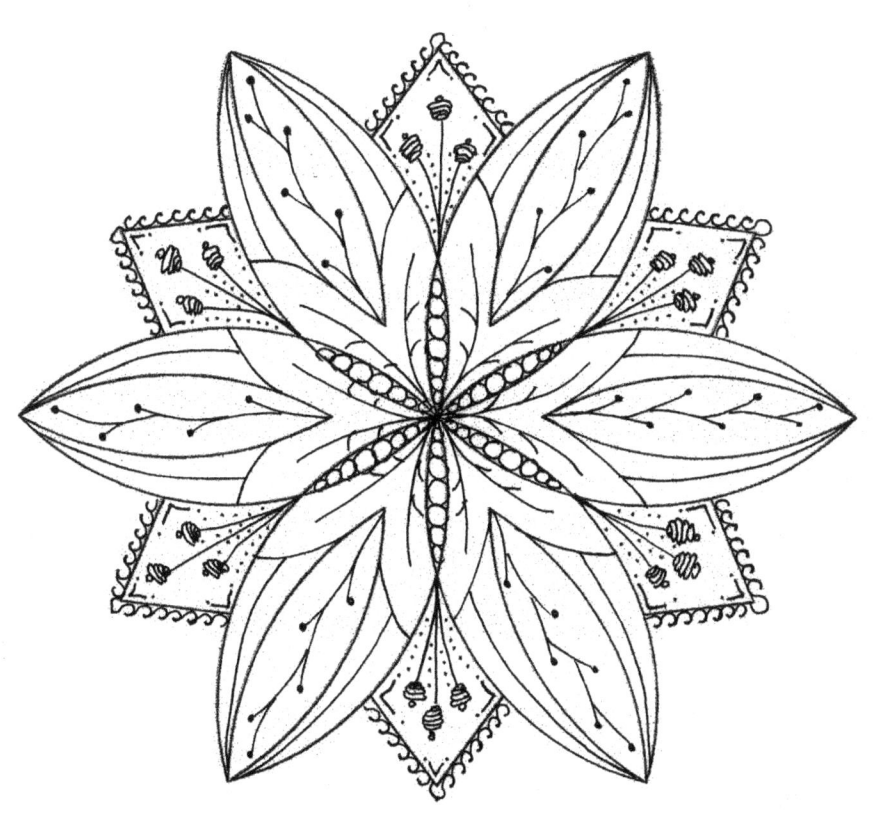

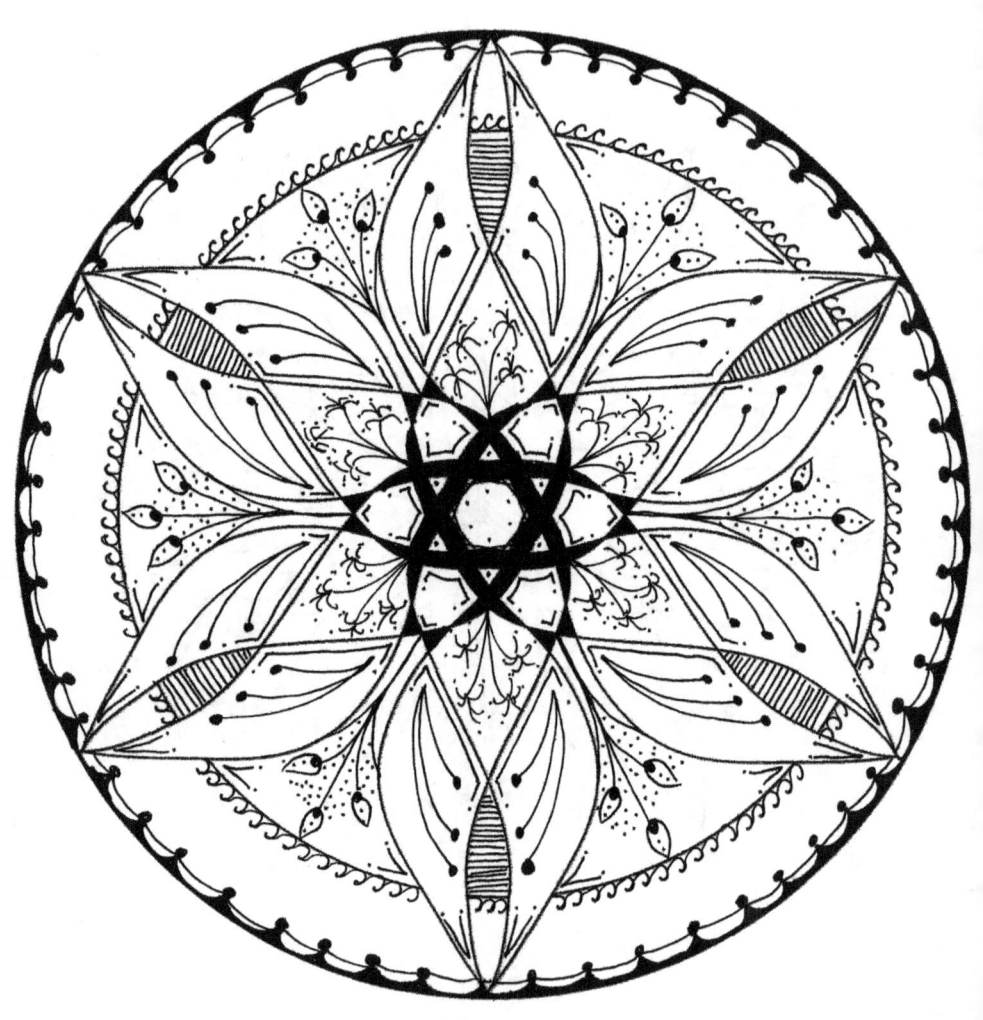

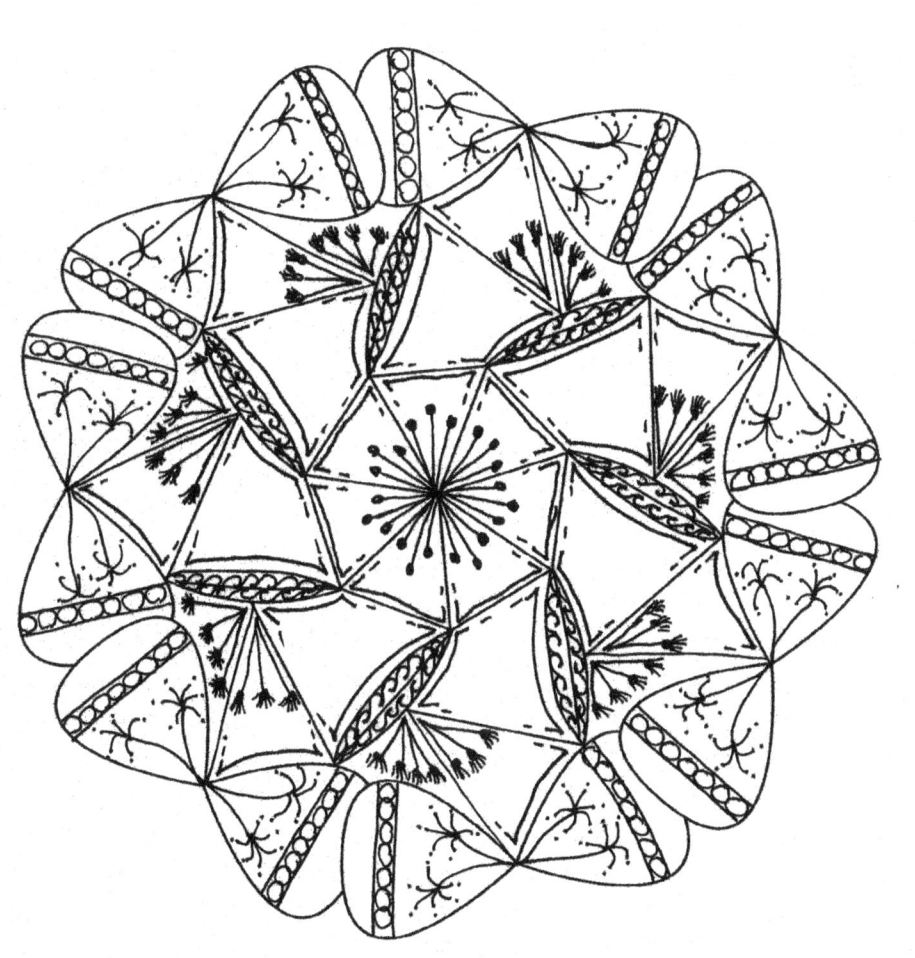

Test your medium!

Pages to test your medium of choice!

www.ingramcontent.com/pod-product-compliance
Lightning Source LLC
Chambersburg PA
CBHW070340190526
45169CB00005B/1984

Louis Figuier

L'Aluminium

Les Merveilles de la science

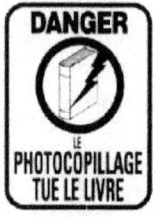
ISBN : 978-1533416513

10 9 8 7 6 5 4 3 2 1